Back On The Road Again

A Personal Journey

Sequel to Airbags and Starting Over

Karen Pivott

www.amazon.com/author/karenpivott

BY THE SAME AUTHOR

BOOKS ON KINDLE

NON FICTION

Airbags and Starting Over

Back On the Road Again
Always Travel With Your Basket

CHILDRENS FICTION

Birthdays at the Bay

Royce and Billy

FICTION

By Any Other Circumstances

Create Space Publishing
4900 LaCross Road
North Charleston, SC 29406
USA

First Printing, Create Space 2016

ISBN-9780473311018

Published in New Zealand

FOREWORD

I wrote this book   because since completing Airbags and Starting over I have realised that there is more to be told.

Change that occurred at that time has been the catalyst to more learning new experiences, and the dogged path now I am back on the road of life again.

The road of life that we are all on. The daily road.

Knowledge gained should be knowledge shared.

Read on and grow.....

Contents

ACKNOWLEDGMENTS

I acknowledge here that my journey has not been endured alone. Without my husband Alan and his ongoing support my books would not be possible. He has encouraged me and loved me throughout all the change, expected and unexpected.

My heartfelt thanks.

Chapter 1. The Everyday Moments

Just over three years on from our car accident and it is the little things which I treasure the most. Things that prior to the accident I didn't notice or give any credence, or attention to, much less acknowledge them as being important, or of some value.

The little things that make my life incredibly rich now. A huge turnaround. Like having a break and talking with my husband.

I was sitting down having a quiet cup of coffee with my husband and we were discussing our day. Mine was quite different to his. This got me thinking about how in our everyday life we cannot know what the people in our lives are actually doing. So how can that be? Let's take a step back. Ask yourself this question. How open are you with the people around you?

Transparent? Guarded? Selective?

Now I am not suggesting you walk around so open that you leave yourself vulnerable, but I am suggesting that you look at how much of yourself you are giving to others. In my experience, and it is only my experience, once you open up more to your nearest and dearest, the more comfortable they are to open up to you, and that is where real communication begins.

Anyone who has raised teenagers and survived the teenage years will know, there are times when you really do not want to know what has occurred, but you really do need to know what is either happening, or has happened so you can take the appropriate action around the situation, for your family. Not all families operate in the same way so finding what is right for you is critical.

How can we survive with the rough and tumble of life? I am no expert but what I know is this; if you are not talking to each other in the good or peaceful times, there is not going to be good communication in the more challenging times, so my suggestion would be start talking to the people you love and care about today. Be honest in what you say, open to what you hear, and above all do not be judgmental or dismissive. Employ active listening, think before you speak, do not be reactive, give yourself time to answer, then reap the rewards.

Active Listening

What is Active Listening? This is a question my learners ask me all the time. It sounds quite technical doesn't it?

For me it is a conscious decision to listen to what is said. To all of what is being said not just bits of it. Listen concentrate and think about what is said, checking that what you are hearing is what is being said and meant, by the person talking.

Don't be afraid to ask questions to check that what you are hearing is what the speaker is meaning.

Be aware that your body language is part of your communication to the speaker, so make sure you are paying attention to what is being said. If you are gazing into the distance clearly your attention is not on the person speaking.

Listen up!

Is it the issue being spoken about or you?

You are sitting in group meeting; A debrief is happening about a recent happening or event and someone says something negative about an activity you were running. You may find yourself a) glaring at the person who is speaking, b) embarrassed, c) feeling marginalized, d) picked on e) not too worried.

In general terms if you are in the e) category of not too concerned you have realized that the speaker is referring to an issue. That is to say you have heard that what is being spoken about is how something, an activity or whatever needs to be done differently.

If you have reacted in the a), b), c), or d), categories it is possible that you have not heard the issue. Your name has been spoken out loud and you have stopped listening to the information at that point.

Be very sure that what you hear is what the issue actually is. You can do that simply by paraphrasing what you have heard and asking for a clarification such as; "So are you saying I had the pricing wrong?

Speaker: "No I am saying that we need to look at our pricing. Is our pricing relevant to what

other fund raisers charge when they sell their
Jams? Comments were made that the
amount of jam was very generous considering
the price."

Every day habits

Yes I have habits and I have learned to use
new habits. One of these is that I am more
thankful every day. I wake up and work hard
all day like most people, the difference
between the, post and pre-accident me is this.
I no longer work hard all day, every day, to be
thankful at the end of the day.

Gobbledygook?

Not really. If we are working hard to find
something to be thankful for then the question
is have we done enough work on ourselves? I
am putting this out there because I have
found that the more work I have done on
myself the more things I have to be thankful
for at the beginning, during and at the end of
every day.

I only look at the next thing to do and get on
with it. I no longer fret about what may be. I
am thankful for a positive outcome before an
event or happening whether that is a family
gathering, a business meeting, a tutoring
session, or writing a book.

"And in all things give thanks"........

Why have we been given this instruction do you think?

Obviously because the more we are thankful the more things we have to be thankful for.

In all things give thanks doesn't need to be a negative message as some of us have been taught in the past.

Give thanks in all things is just that, an instruction to give thanks in all things. We don't have to second guess or analyse it just do it. That is something we can all do every day and easily.

Do you love getting things you've wanted?

The best and easiest way to get what you want or what you love is to be thankful for it. When you see it be thankful. Yes even before you physically have it in your possession.

If you are in a less than ideal situation and you want to come out of it in a better space or place, then be thankful for the good result you've received, and believe you have received it.

It can be very enlightening to try this out. The Manager or colleague who is driving you nuts? The child who is pushing boundaries. Great opportunities to put thankfulness into action. Be thankful before you meet with them or have an important discussion with them, and be thankful once the encounter has ended.

Will you get a great result straight away? Yes. Maybe. Later. Not at all on occasion, but something different will happen to what has been happening beforehand. Why?

Well two things have happened. You have been thankful (1) and expected a good result (2) so you will have communicated differently, verbally and non-verbally.

Try it a few times and the more you practice this the more often you will see the results you want.

Chapter 2. Family Matters

For the purpose of this chapter I am referring to family matters as significant events or happenings in the lives of family members, yours, not other peoples. I used to find myself embroiled or pickled in these happenings when I was younger, but I have learned thankfully to offer advice if asked, and keep out of the brouhaha when it does not concern me.

I really don't need to know all the belly hoo and dirty tid bits. They make for good entertainment in movies, television, and plays, but in real life it really is like dosing embers with oxygen so they can reignite extending the pain, attention, and resolution out further than it needs to be.

Yes I can hear you the but......

I agree with you absolutely, the only but, that
is relevant if it is not your business directly, is
to BUTT right out, and leave it to those
involved to sort. They were there at the start
and they will be there somewhere at the end,
but where that somewhere is quite frankly is
up to them.

I have had daughter in laws I have loved to
bits, but that does not help when a marriage
is coming unstuck. Two people get married,
two people get divorced. One of our children
was in the mix and I intended to still have that
child in my life at the end of the day.

This may sound harsh, but I came to realize
that I had invested a lot of time, patience, love
and guidance over years in that child, and
through that time had accepted like everyone,
that children are not perfect. Whatever
reasons may be given and shouted from the
roof tops, there are always two people involved
in a marriage, or relationship so those two
people have to sort it out, not three or more.

Divorce is the extreme end of the scale. The
ructions can well start with the planning of
the wedding so to speak. At the start of an
event when everyone has to have their say,
and their point of view is more important than

everyone else's. What interests me with this is the person who generally, and I am generalizing here, has the most to say about what you should want , have or do, will be the very person who gets everything they want, how they want it, when they want it, most of the time regardless of what you or others might say.

Managing yourself

In my view and from what I have observed to date over many years the best way you can help in either situation is to manage yourself and keep yourself in check. If you are asked for advice and it is valid offer it up then let it go. What happens to that advice after you have given it is over to the person or people who have asked for it. They get to decide. Not you.

If you are asked what do you think, and you can see that what you think is not going to advance the situation just say something like "You seem to be on track so I have nothing really to offer at this time." Or "I don't' feel it is my place to say anything right now."

Keeping your composure

This is an area where I have been known to struggle in my personal and work life. I often find myself starting to react to what is happening around me, and in those situations it can be very easy to lose my composure.

I have learned to distract myself to a degree when things are heating up around me, or people are being very opinionated and this does help. I have found a very useful strategy is to go to the toilet or leave the room and find a quiet area and do some tapping on the point of contention.

When you are hit with the unexpected news

My colleague and I were on our way back to work after a long session in a rural location when my personal cell phone rang. This I might say is very unusual so I answered it. A garbled and upset voice was spluttering and I asked "Your brother has broken his arm?"

Our eight year old grandson some 1500 kilometers away was ringing to tell me of his accident. Dad's interjection on the line clarified that it was the grandson on the phone, not his brother who had broken his arm. Once that was cleared up the conversation started to make a bit more sense. The explanation that he was flying off the monkey bars at school, landing awkwardly on his left arm, and my arm hurts and looks funny, brought the image clearly into focus

for me. It was revealed later that night that he had done a very good job of the breakage.
Two bones broken in three places.

In the car though I was not a very composed lady. I felt sick, my heart began racing and I felt completely useless. My colleague who was driving the car was very supportive throughout the unfolding conversation. Once I had spoken to his dad I had more of an idea about what was happening next.

By the end of a very long night, surgery and plastered up our grandson was realigned and on the road to recovery, by which time I was much more composed than I had been earlier in the day.

Keep it real

Many of us can find ourselves in these situations. My colleague said at the time "You handled that so well, and he feels so much better for talking to you."

 Now I was not processing any of that at the time, and that is my point. Yes we may not always respond in the most appropriate way all the time, but then we are not always getting the news or information we are expecting. Beating yourself up over a reaction to something unexpected is quite normal. We need time to process what has happened and to work out what we need to do next if anything. Continuing to react inappropriately by casting blame, having an opinion which is not helpful, or any other negative behaviour in the situation is not okay.

Often in these situations we revert to the "old me". A good test of how far you have come is in these very situations.

I ask myself these questions:

- Am I helping or hindering?
- Am I being supportive or judgmental?
- Am I being too hard on myself?

Chapter 3. Personal Growth

Nothing happens in isolation and I have come to learn and accept that what I think, often determines what is going to come next. I will give you a good well accepted, and widely known example of this. I break a glass in the morning and my husband says "Well you know what they say things happen in threes."

Now let's have a look at this. I have broken a glass. Singular. How is my breaking a glass in itself going to create another two negative events happening?

Some time ago I would have accepted that and carried on and when the next thing broke or bad news arrived I would put that down to the second of the third thing having occurred.

Then when the third thing happened I would be relieved because that was the three things that had happened and now I was free and clear. What's more I was expecting and accepting all this as if it was real. Really?

Yes really, and we all do this all the time when we buy into the beliefs of others. Yes beliefs. This is a belief. The belief is that when one thing goes wrong three things will go wrong, and we believe it so it happens. Simple as that.

This is what I know today: I break a glass in the morning. I clean up the mess and I get on with my day. A singular event cleaned up and left in the bin.

How did I get here? I have turned off the tape in my head and no longer hear the reinforcing chatter of past beliefs. I cannot tell you how freeing that is.

Bob Proctor covers this subject well as does Dr. Joe Vitale, Natalie Ledwell and others so there is lots of information out there.

Breaking the barriers

So how did I get here did I just flick the switch? Yes but it took a lot of reading, a lot of processing and a lot of faith in my ability, and my resolve to walk away from what I had learned. To begin learning a new way, which thankfully for me has meant a much higher quality of life, better outcomes, better work/life balance. The courage to share my learned skills and observations of life with many people. To help people improve the quality of their own lives, and the lives of their family and wider community.

Why is this so important? Initially I just wanted to sort myself out and experience more of the positive things life has to offer rather than the negative things we believe we should be accepting.

It turns out that positive lives are infectious. I kid you not. If you had the choice between spending 12 hours in a dark room with a positive person or a negative person. Which one would you choose?

Think about the times you've spent in a meeting with a person who is positive or optimistic. In my experience the time passes very quickly. By contrast when you are in a meeting with a pessimist or a negative person the time seems to drag on. More than that there seems to be an additional weight in the room or a cloud dragging the atmosphere of the room down. Are we aware of this at the time? Most people are aware of something not being quite right because they often feel it or sense it.

One of the things we can do is have positive thoughts about the meeting before we go in and expect a positive result. When you get very specific about what you want or need and believe you have received it you will find it is much easier to be positive and your behaviour will reflect this. As I said earlier it turns out positive lives are infectious and so are positive thoughts. Thoughts alone won't do it, but they do allow you to be more open to the resources you need to pull things together. Resources being the right information, the right people, the right timing.

Just recently I needed something and was totally focused on it. The first thing I did was make a list of what I would need including the time it may take. Next I prioritized my list and made an action plan or to put it another way I put things into order. The last step was taking action while being focused on the outcome. My outcomes overall have improved dramatically.

Using the new way

Once you have learned a new way of doing something you need to actually start using it.

It's easy for you to say, you may be thinking. Yes it is because I started doing things differently. Not just reading about them, not just listening to speakers or watching motivational videos actually doing what I was learning.

Thought + Action = Outcome

Once you change your thoughts and take new actions you will effect better outcomes for yourself and others. Using the new way often is the best way to start seeing the benefits of your personal growth in real terms.

Personal growth comes from application and the easiest way to accelerate personal growth is to consciously decide to use the new way until it becomes your way.

Moving forward

Once you are using the new way you are by default moving in a different direction. Do not be surprised if that feels at times like going sideways or backwards. You have a brain with a memory and that brain will continue to tell you "you should be doing it this way or the old way". This in turn puts your brain into conflict as it were with itself. Continuing to use the new way is the key to relaxing your brain and have your brain accept that this is "the way". The new normal so to speak.

Trial and error is a part of this, as is some frustration. Be bold, focused and steadfast and you will reap the rewards. I have been back on the road again for over three years and I still have the odd day when my brain is telling me to do the old. I do not comply. I do and use the new, and I am way better off for doing so. Good luck and persevere.

There is the saying "fake it till you make it." I prefer "do it till until it is you."

Memory and the role it plays

I've just told you to move on and do things the new way and now I am bringing up the memory thing in more detail. Why?

If you have ever had an operation when you are awake throughout you will know you can feel the pressure of everything. The pain may be muted but the pressure is still present.

Many years ago I had a series of eye operations which always started with the eye being numbed by way of drops, and these drops stung quite badly. Now when I say many years ago I am talking 40 years ago and although that happened then, when I go to my optometrist and have an eye exam involving drops, my eyes think they were attacked by the stinging drops yesterday.

This never made sense to me. I can allow the drops to go in. I even reduce my anxiety before the test is done, but the minute I see the drops coming my eyes shut. I have been threatened with having my eyes forced open and I have not agreed to that.

Then on one occasion my Optometrist said to me "I would tell you to relax or look away but that is not going to work."

"What do we do then?" I asked him.

"We tell your eye these drops are cold but won't sting and if that doesn't work you can put them in yourself." And he left the room.

"I sat and thought about this and rationalized that as the drops had come out of the fridge then of course they would be cold, and if worse came to worse I could put them in as he suggested."

He duly returned with the drops, I looked up he said "Now they will be cold but just cold." Voila drops in no problem.

After the test I spoke to him about this having apologized for protracting the process and he said simply, "No need to apologize my dear. Eyes have a memory and they are doing what they are designed to do. Protect themselves."

I have never forgotten that, and each time I have to have that test done I remind my eyes that these drops are the cold ones and it will be fine. I wish I could say we have the one drop hit rate each time, but that would be a stretch. We do however have the within the normal time frame range so that is fine by me and no anxiety.

What I am getting at here is that a memory can be acknowledged, and accepted but a change can still occur. A memory does not have to scar us or hold us back in our life. It is our past. It resides in our past. It happened but each day we are creating or experiencing new events which become memories of their own, and the good ones are just as irrelevant as the old ones in terms of the present. They have happened and they too are in the past.

Chapter 4. Concepts of Time

I have talked a bit about the past, present and future which are measures of time in a timeframe.

We as people work with time frames all the time. Day and night. Morning, afternoon, evening. Hours of work. Shift work. School timetables. Study times. Shopping hours. The list is endless.

To organize ourselves in terms of keeping to deadlines or working in a timely manner we can create lists, use a calendar, diary or journal.

For all our efforts and energy though there is in reality only one time and that is the present.

Yes we can create our present as it were over time by projecting what we want now for the future, but we function in the contemporary time. We are and live in the present.

The past is gone it no longer exists in real time. The future may be seen or projected, but in real terms it is not here yet so it does not exist.

The present is here and it is in the present we must learn to focus ourselves.

Wasting time thinking about the past is just that. By all means as I have said before acknowledge the past if it helps you in the present. Brooding about the past though just robs you of productive time in the present and the present is important.

Using our time well

My work colleague of many years had a card on her desk saying this "The present is a gift." Now if we look at this saying and belief we can see that the present is given to us 'a gift'. We are entrusted with this gift over and over again and as with all gifts there is a degree of expectation, gratitude and joy or disappointment.

Often around present giving we will hear "It's the thought that counts."

If we look at this saying what leaps out to me is the question. How much time has been given to the thought?

There are times of course when you see something and you just know, that what you have seen is the perfect gift for a particular person, and to act on that there and then is a very good thing.

If someone requests a gift card and you honour that request that is also a good thing. I have grandchildren who love receiving a gift card because they can choose what they get, and tend to wait for the sales to go shopping.

Is this a cop out? I don't think so because there has been discussion and agreement.

Is this a good use of time? Yes.

What I have learned over the years is how to maximize the effective use of time, and what I have found is this. It is the simple things that make the difference. Simple things and the application of them.

I am a list person and this saves me heaps of time. I fill out a list of what I have to do the following day, and have it ready for the morning. If I am writing for example I will set aside time to write. Now that may require me to get up earlier, but the writing will be done for the day, then I move onto the next thing on my list.

For young people the use of a timer on their phone will keep them on track whereas I use an analogue clock.

All the jobs that have to be done are prioritized in order of importance and time appropriateness. By time appropriateness I mean when you can actually do them.

For example if my list is set up; writing 0600; shopping 0900; it is because the shops do not open until 0900.

During the festive season shops are often open much later than usual so shopping times can be extended.

Put some time into your day for exercise. I walk after work in the early evening before dinner or potter in my garden. If you don't have time for this or the gym perhaps increase the amount of walking or standing you do in the day. Get off you chair and move if you can.

Once you work to lists or prioritise your lists you notice immediately that you seemingly have more free or spare time and I love that. What is really happening here? You are managing activity. Time is constant.

Having lists makes me focus and keeps me on track. If you use them you need to remain focused, and on track to get results, and only you can do that. I know young people who have digital diaries or electronic calendar schedules that serve them just as well.

Likewise having a list can ensure that when you have to meet someone socially, for example morning tea, you have the time you have set aside to focus on and enjoy them. No distractions, no interruptions. Yes turn those phones off, relax and enjoy. The world won't end, but you will have sent it a very powerful message.

This is my time and I am using it well.

Other tips: When you go somewhere and you know you will be waiting for someone else take something you can do with you while you are waiting.

When I was young there was a woman who sat in the badminton hall. While her children played she crocheted rugs for charity. She used to produce about twenty a year. Read a book. Take some study with you.

I have recently discovered audio books and you can put them onto an MP3 player and listen to your heart's content while you are watching and waiting on the side lines.

One of my learner's years ago practiced his writing while he was waiting for his truck to be unloaded. He was unloaded 8 to 10 times a day. His writing improved exponentially. I am not kidding. He is now a Supervisor.

Technology does have its place, and we can use it to our advantage, but technology can also distract us and many hours are lost because of this.

The best thing I can say is this;

Know that you and you alone can maximize your own time whether that is at work, at home, at school, in the community, with family, or with friends.

Maximize your effectiveness and enjoy your down time. It is all about balance and the more balanced you are the better you are in all things. Your health improves. Your productivity improves. Your self- esteem improves. You improve.

Remember: Once time has gone we do not get it back.

Chapter 5. Letting People Be Themselves and Move to Their Own Groove

Yes this chapter has a long title which is uncharacteristic for this writer but appropriate. I say appropriate because for me this has been one of the lessons which has taken me the longest time to learn.

In my previous book "Airbags and Starting Over" I spoke about the frustration of being the person who phones people and those people don't always ring back. After several calls and no answers I have to remind myself why I am calling that person.

I have a particular person who has an answer machine that tells you every time you ring "Leave your name and number and we will get right back to you." Only they don't get right back to people.

Am I suggesting they have a message like "Leave your name and number and if we think you are worth calling back we will?" No of course not. Just be aware that when people ring you and leave a message multiple times, they either may need to talk to you because they need you, or they may have information you need, and if you don't talk to them, they will stop ringing you.

Don't ring someone and apologize and say how hopeless you are because you never get back to them. Disable the answering machine. If the phone keeps ringing and no one answers it then you are not available period. If the answer phone picks up and asks someone to leave a message the expectation is that the person will be answered. Answer phones weren't invented to be a screening device.

What does all this have to do with 'Letting People Be Themselves and Move to Their Own Groove'? Simply this. There does come a point when you as a person move on from being dismissed or side lined in someone else's life. Take it from me when the messages stopped being left, and people stop phoning completely, and the months roll by, sooner or later a person will come to the inevitable conclusion that, if they want someone in their life, they have to do something as well.

It is the give and take scenario. If you keep giving and others keep taking, they will not only keep taking but expect to be given to all the time, and that is not how give and take is meant to work.

As with communication, friendship, work life, there needs to be give and take. Two way traffic.

What I have learned is that for some people who have had people in their lives who have always done the majority of the work, or phoning, writing, keeping in touch, giving them information, doing their research, yes the list is endless. Those people now feel entitled to be receivers on their terms and that is not okay.

When these people stop receiving, and their world begins to slow and parts of it die off completely, they then realise that they need to take action.

This has happened recently to a friend of mine who over time has relied on others to chase her up, arrange dinners, shopping trips, phone her, and all of a sudden she has come to the conclusion that if she doesn't contact some of her friends they will have moved on without her.

How did she get to this point? It started with messages not being left on her answer phone, then people stopped ringing her, stopped texting her, stopped emailing her because they never got a reply. People stopped asking her along to things because she would never confirm with them whether or not she was coming.

How do I know this? She rang me and told me she wasn't invited to something but knew it had happened without her. The sad thing about this situation is that the person really likes to be involved but on her terms.

This lady is now phoning and catching up with her friends because she has realised she needs them, and it was a lesson that took her years to learn. Another six months down the track and she may have found that she had left it a bit late.

A big part of letting people move to their own groove is to let them be. Yes let them be.

Here is an example:

If someone says something to you about someone else you can do one of three things a) Ignore it. b) Check with, the someone else. c) Go blindly along and get caught up in someone else's groove, and yes you will get stuck there.

If you are not happy with the way they are behaving just get on with your own life and dare I say it move to your own groove. There are times when people come into our lives for a reason and we do lots with them and then they are gone.

Sometimes there is a very good reason for that as well, so let them go and keep moving to your own groove.

What I have learned is that rest periods between the people passing through, coming or going in our lives is perfectly okay. We are fluid beings not static that is why we grow.

We do not have to be relying on, held back or used by others. We just need to get on with our own life, trusting the little voice inside, and it will all work out.

How do I know this?

I am seeing things happening around me and to me, and those things are a mixture as life is, and at the end of the day it works out. Not always how I may have thought originally, but I am richer as a result. Not financially richer, but richer in myself and that is a very good place to be.

Accepting no as the answer

It is not so easy to say NO. I have had to learn how to do it and it took me ages. What is less easy for some people is to accept NO as an answer.

I bring this up here because this is another example of 'Let People Be Themselves and Move to Their Own Groove'.

For some people the thought of having to find a replacement or work with someone new is just too much so they rely on the status quo because it works, or they are comfortable with it, or they are in control of it, then you come along and say NO I am not able to do this anymore and the guilt, pleading, snub, or any other inappropriate behaviour may rear its ugly head.

For many people who have a winning team around them, or a situation where they are excelling in the role they have because of the people around them, the word NO is an immediate threat to their current position and there may well be a reaction.

Until recently I had not given this much thought. But when I announced I was no longer going to do a job which was an extra the first visible reaction was anger rather than disappointment. So I worked with the person

to find a successor and extricated myself
successfully from that job.

What I learned through this was that not
everyone has the same skill set and
sometimes people need to learn something
new and often on committees, or in
workplaces the people relying on the job to be
done do not have the time to work through the
transitional period of the changeover. That
said one person saying NO and that being
accepted, allows for others to have the
opportunity to take over, and although we
don't all do the same thing the same way, so
long as the job is done does it really matter?

I struggled with something for quite some
time and asked to be relinquished from that
job. In the end I stated I was not going to do it
because....

The person who took over that job complained
on their first day and they did not have any of
my issues to deal with.

Some may say I am a slow learner. Too kind.
Too soft. A pushover. Some of that may be
true. The absolute truth however was that I
was allowing someone else to dictate what I
would be doing, when I knew it was causing
me harm and that is not okay.

I have learned that not only is that behaviour

on both sides not okay I was able to take steps to stop it continuing.

Never feel threatened by someone not taking NO for an answer if necessary deliver the message a different way.

Remember when you say NO you know you are going to be saying NO, the person receiving the message is not expecting to get it, so a little space or practical suggestion can often soften the delivery.

Moving on

When something has ended the expectation is that we move on, or in some cases move over.

What I have experienced over time is that people do this at different times and at different speeds.

Allowing someone the space to move on in their own time is a true indication that you have got to a place where you understand fully what 'Let People Be Themselves and Move To, Their Own Groove' means.

We may have a plan in place to help through the change, but other people even when the change has occurred seem to struggle with the reality of their new found situation. Yes even when they know it is going to happen.

Some of the most capable people I know have at times struggled with this. Whether it is the fear of the unknown. The reality that what they have strived for is actually happening and the fear of not being good enough occurs.

Whatever the reason patience is required and often listening does a lot more good than talking.

Comments such as "but you knew this was going to happen." Or "I thought this is what you wanted." Are not going to be helpful. Remember the "Managing yourself" excerpt the same rules apply here.

then you find yourself with huge stress, frustration and expense.

Whether it is in the criminal, civil, family or employment arena the only thing I can say is this: If you know you are in the right and you know like you know, like you know you have done nothing wrong holding onto to that knowledge will sustain you regardless of the outcome reached by the judiciary. Know also that adjudicators, police, judges, facilitators, bosses and others are also human beings, and they can get things wrong. Yes they can and do make mistakes, and even though those mistakes are costly to the wronged party, forgiveness for those errors is something I recommend. Being able to forgive those who seem to be bashing the bashed will bring you relief, clarity of mind, and allow you to move forward. Where to? How? I have no idea and in that moment neither will you that is my experience. The realization that you still have not been heard is one of utter disbelief in my experience, followed by shock, a descending fog, followed by some anger then frustration and the cycle of the downward spiral is taking perfect shape. The road to moving forward is to erase it all in your mind and clear it away. Even your feelings will dissipate and neutralize altogether if you do the following: Forgive those who have wronged you initially and subsequent people who have come along and followed them. Know that if you have been wronged God sees all that, and put your trust in him. He will bring you through it.

Is it scary when you are facing huge bills? Absolutely.

Is it unfair? Yes.

Is it unjust? Yes.

Are you going to be defined by it? Only you can answer that but for me the answer is an absolute no. Life goes on and I intend to continue engaging with life. Don't allow yourself to get stuck. Being stuck is extremely uncomfortable no matter how large the space or great the view, because no matter what you try you cannot move forward. You need to move forward and move on or past that point.

Making the most of given situations

Whatever the situation you find yourself in, or whatever side of it you may be on always be true to yourself, and do not do anything you may regret when it is over. Honesty is the best policy. Truth is the best tool always because once you tell the truth you can recall it over and over again. Lies start catching you out so I would advise not ever going there, even if your truth has not been believed no one can take your truth away from you.

Even in trying circumstances or events you will emerge with something positive you didn't know about yourself or others.

That inner voice will emerge and give you the strength, encouragement, information or inspiration to carry you on. Our inner voice can be used to great effect. In some cases it can even warn you of danger.

Stopping the tape in your head

Yes this is possible. I have found self-hypnosis tapes useful of late, but prior to that I have found that accepting what has happened then setting it free extremely useful.

"Be still and know I am God."

This was told to me as a child. As a child I thought it meant close your eyes and pray. Close the world out in other words.

As an Adult I realise it takes much more than that. You need to be consciously aware of where you are, and what you are doing, then consciously bring yourself to a place of stillness. There are many ways to get there.

I use a clearing technique and find myself using this technique more and more, so that when I am still my mind is clear and free.

Other techniques that I have found useful for positive and negative thoughts and feelings;

Visualisation. For me I have a big dump truck that I climb aboard. I load a big bucket or scoop on the front and I drive head on in to the negative situation scoop it up and deposit it over the bank to my left where all negative things go never to be seen or heard of again.

For the smaller things that come up I have canisters that I take to the swirling grey matter and entice them into the canister then promptly empty the canister over the side of the bank to the left. They also go to the place where they are never seen or heard again.

Each time negative anything appears I do this now. Things do still come up, but they get smaller and smaller each time until my mind no longer thinks of or acknowledges them again and they truly are gone.

Persevere with this and you will find a life less cluttered with negative thoughts and memories.

This may sound odd and it does take some practice, but I have found this extremely healing and I follow it up by loving the person anyway, forgiving them and thanking them for what I have learned.

 I then think of a time when I was happy and smile very broadly.

I also have a system for seeing good things coming to me. I have a large cart deliver the things I want, deposit them into the good for you bank and watch the good things appear on a very large well lit board to my right.

My cart is purple with yellow writing outlined in red saying congratulations Karen you have received.

Again this has taken practice, and I am very excited when the alarm goes off and I receive a delivery. Excited and grateful and I smile a lot. I feel warm inside and very happy when this happens and I have found that I am more relaxed each time I receive. More relaxed and more comfortable with my successes and winnings.

My cart is winched away with the words "Until next time enjoy" and I do.

Breathing exercises help you to relax, afford you clarity and stillness of mind making your pictures vibrant and easy to engage with.

Meditation is useful and I use guided meditation at least three times a week. Some people do this every day.

Tapping or EFT is a good stress reliever as well.

However you get there, know that when you are there, the way forward or a deep sense of inner peace will come to you. That has been my experience to date, and it is great.

Make Believe

Am I going nuts? Some may think so, but I believe in the make believe world because we are using it every day before we are told it is make believe. When we are young we can accomplish things that at times defy gravity.

Climbing a tree and getting stuck, then coming down safely when logically we should never have been able to a) get that high in the first place b)stay on a branch too light safely c) getting down to ground level safely again.

We see ourselves climbing up the tree and climb up the tree. We see ourselves sitting on the branch. We see ourselves climbing down again unscathed. We expect to do it without a problem so we do just that.

The world of make believe is a safe one for you. Explore it and see what you want clearly. The how you get there is not up to you, but things do come to you in the real world. Make believe is also a good way of turning off the tape that runs and pops up in your mind from time to time. The more often you 'make believe' the less time the tape is on.

Chapter 6. Injustices

This is a subject I have plenty of personal knowledge on, and I can tell you from personal experience that even when you follow the legal path justice unfortunately is not guaranteed, and then you find yourself with huge stress, frustration and expense.

Whether it is in the criminal, civil, family or employment arena the only thing I can say is this: If you know you are in the right and you know like you know, like you know you have done nothing wrong holding onto to that knowledge will sustain you regardless of the outcome reached by the judiciary. Know also that adjudicators, police, judges, facilitators, bosses and others are also human beings, and they can get things wrong. Yes they can and do make mistakes, and even though those mistakes are costly to the wronged party, forgiveness for those errors is something I recommend.

Being able to forgive those who seem to be bashing the bashed will bring you relief, clarity of mind, and allow you to move forward. Where to? How? I have no idea and in that moment neither will you that is my experience. The realization that you still have not been heard is one of utter disbelief in my experience, followed by shock, a descending fog, followed by some anger then frustration and the cycle of the downward spiral is taking perfect shape. The road to moving forward is to erase it all in your mind and clear it away. Even your feelings will dissipate and neutralize altogether if you do the following: Forgive those who have wronged you initially and subsequent people who have come along and followed them. Know that if you have been wronged God sees all that, and put your trust in him. He will bring you through it.

Is it scary when you are facing huge bills? Absolutely.

Is it unfair? Yes.

Is it unjust? Yes.

Are you going to be defined by it? Only you

can answer that but for me the answer is an absolute no. Life goes on and I intend to continue engaging with life. Don't allow yourself to get stuck. Being stuck is extremely uncomfortable no matter how large the space or great the view, because no matter what you try you cannot move forward. You need to move forward and move on or past that point.

Making the most of given situations

Whatever the situation you find yourself in, or whatever side of it you may be on always be true to yourself, and do not do anything you may regret when it is over. Honesty is the best policy. Truth is the best tool always because once you tell the truth you can recall it over and over again. Lies start catching you out so I would advise not ever going there, even if your truth has not been believed no one can take your truth away from you.

Even in trying circumstances or events you will emerge with something positive you didn't know about yourself or others.

That inner voice will emerge and give you the strength, encouragement, information or inspiration to carry you on. Our inner voice can be used to great effect. In some cases it can even warn you of danger.

Chapter 7. When You Are Facing the Loss of A Loved One

Loss is something that we all face from time to time across a multitude of areas in our lives. The longer we live the more likely we are to face loss.

Once you know you are going to lose something or someone the dealing with the loss phase begins.

For most people this happens in stages, and like grief the stages people go through are not all in the same order. Similarly the timeframes may also vary.

Some people accept what is happening or

about to happen, and just get on with things. They may make a plan of things to do. People to contact. Places to visit. Some people keep themselves busy. Other people can deny it is happening and don't appear to deal with it at all. While still some others get angry and vocal, or act out, or blame, or perform a myriad of actions while they come to terms with what is about to go, or has gone already.

Some people never seem to bounce back or recover to their former state. Still others over time can come through the loss and find themselves moving in a new direction, or seem at peace with where they are.

When you find yourself walking alongside someone who is going through this process you need to give them room. Room to find out which road they are going to take and be supportive. You need to ensure they do not descend into dark places for too long, and seek medical intervention if you have concerns about them.

If you are facing sudden loss or are on notice that you going to lose something or someone get help or support if you need it. There is nothing embarrassing or shameful about asking for support. I myself have learned this, and have found that once the truth is out there people will be there for you. Very possibly you have been there for others in the past yourself.

What I have learned to my detriment is that the longer you try to handle things alone you end up not doing yourself any favors at all.

In fact you can be cutting yourself off from the people who do care about you, or make things worse for yourself because you don't have objective advice with how to resolve matters.

A recent conversation with one of our children went like this "I have learned it is the people who will have the tough honest conversations with you when you don't want to have or hear them and that two things are true. 1) Deep down you already know you should be doing whatever or accepting that what you are doing is not okay. 2) The people who are having the tough conversations with you are people you really want to have in your life because they are there for you. They love you. They care about you. They accept you. They see what you need to do to benefit you and have the guts to speak up.

Dealing with the reality of it all

This is the mucky phase. You are wading through the mire so to speak. The daily grind of getting up and doing what is necessary as well as dealing with the loss on top of that.

One day at a time. Every minute of every day.
Day after day. Many people feel they are in a
fog, tunnel or vortex with no way out. No
matter what they do they feel swamped or
powerless.

These feelings are normal. If they carry on for
too long though you may need help or arrange
for the person to get some medical attention.
This could be just a check-up or some
treatment options may be explored or
prescribed for the person.

My grandfather used to say things like "It's
not the war it's the daily grind of finding
yourself on the move but still in the war. No
respite." When you are eight you don't know
what that means, but what I did know was
that he didn't much like it. Not from what he
was saying, but from the way he was saying it.
He had no choice in the matter. He was there
and had to do what he was told to do.

What loss and my grandfather's war have in
common is the journey through before the end
is reached. That is the reality. The end
doesn't just turn up waving a flag at the start
of the loss telling you "I am here and you have
found me and you are going to be all right."

As in everything apply yourself to the loss and
what it means for you the best you can every

day. Do not beat yourself up if you have
some bad days. There are over three hundred
days in a year you are allowed to have a few
less good ones.

Being Positive

Strange heading when you are facing loss I
admit, but even small gains need to be
recognized and acknowledged. Enjoying the
small things is a big part of recovery.

The feel of the sun on your skin. Going for a
small walk. Dressing using colour when your
instincts are to surround yourself with
comforting black or dull clothing.

Phoning a friend to see what they're doing.
Yes you may be thinking like I care what
they're doing, I'm the one going through the
mire, but here's the thing I have found, it can
be healing to connect with people who are just
getting on with their normal daily things, and
talking about their normal daily things. It
gives you a mental rest from your current
situation.

I am speaking from experience here, and I can
say right here and now hand on heart, to
avoid falling back into your situation you need
to give them the heads up.

"Hi Gayle. I'm just taking a few moments out

to check on how you are doing and this conversation has to stay with what you and yours are doing okay? Let's start with how are the kids?"

Don't mock it until you've tried it. I found that by connecting with the real world still operating outside of my situation kept me connected and gave me a break from the loss I was dealing with. Yes I will admit for a brief period, but those periods lengthened as I began to heal and they will for you too.

One of the things I didn't realise at the beginning of my loss phase was that people wanted to help but didn't know how to. People didn't want to add more to my stress. By phoning them and talking about their day, their family, their job, they felt they were helping me and they were. Popping in followed. They felt able to make short visits and feel comfortable talking about their family, mutual friends and all manner of everyday things, and slowly things began to move to a better rhythm.

Picking up the pace

Once you start to gain a bit of momentum it is important to make steady progress in this area. Try to avoid all out going for it days. You don't want to run out of juice halfway through a meeting, visit or exercising.

Eat well. Cut out junk food and stick to whole foods if you can. Make you sure you drink enough water or non-caffeinated fluid through the day. Try and exercise a bit everyday even if you start by walking partway down your street or around your property. Get out of your living space and clear your head. Even sitting on a porch or balcony with the sun on your face is better than remaining a shut in.

Yes I have been there. Just the thought of going out was a major at the start but in the end I just got out of bed and walked to the mail box. I didn't think about it. I just did it. I found the world was still out there. It was a cold windy day and the rose bushes were moving around, the wind had a real chill factor and my body visibly shuddered, but I continued standing there looking at the empty mailbox, then looking up and down the street before returning to the house to start my day.

By the end of that week I was walking to the short end of the street and back every day. The week after halfway down the street and so on. What I learned by doing this was that I still had control over something. I was no longer as powerless or as helpless as I had thought when I was in the shock phase.

Does it all go back to normal?

What's normal? Does life go back to where it

was before the loss occurred? No. In short how can it? You have gone through something and you will not be the same when you have come through it. Having said that you may find you are actually in a better place. If not you will learn to live with the different place you now find yourself in, and hopefully continue moving forward from there.

What I found was that once I was through the worst of it people came to me, and I was included in gatherings, outings, conversations, and I felt more at ease again.

It is possible to create your new normal and be comfortable with that. The term makeover springs to mind.

Think about a house being made over. The majority of the foundation of the house will be used. Things may look different when it is all finished, but the house is still there at the same address, in the same place on the same piece of land.

We are like that to. We can be made over. The outer projection of ourselves may be a bit different, but the core of us, the essence of who we are is still there.

Chapter 8. Make Plans for a Purposeful Life

This chapter heading is a mouthful. Actually it is a head full because you need to think long and hard about where you are now, where you want to be, and how you are going to get there. Also in the mix is the reflection on where you have been and how you can use those memories to springboard you on this stage of your journey.

Many years ago, and for many years I heard the mantra "there's no point looking back that is done."

I believed that completely which led me to compartmentalize areas, events, and memories of my life very well. Then once those things were safely put away I would move on to the next thing, never looking back.

What I now know after lots of study is that I can revisit the memory and change it to what I had wanted it to be and feel good about it. I have also learned that not all the memories, events or situations are negative. There will be good bits present, and those are what I need to remember so I can look at where it went pear shaped, and determine to read those signals better next time to get a better result, or know when to walk away earlier or change direction, get some help or whatever else I need to get my desired and expected result or outcome.

The reason this works is because I have control of it, and I am looking at the situation as if I am someone else looking over it.

Why do I do this?

I need to stop making the same mistakes over and over again. Why? Simply because I am not getting what I need to be happy and do well in whatever the situations may be.

Recognizing your blocks

For years I believed I could not sit exams and pass. I had been told that by parents and teachers over the years so of course that was real for me.

I worked hard. Studied hard. Got extra help
with my study. Result. Still failed. I was an
A grade student until I sat an exam, and this
trend continued when I returned to school as
an adult student at the age of thirty two, sat
my practice English exam, and had my
English teacher ring me and blow me up over
the phone. That was not only humiliating and
embarrassing it was soul destroying. How did
I change it? I took the initiative and went onto
the offensive and calmly said to my English
teacher "We both know I can do it, I have the
knowledge and I need to pass so what can I
do?"

Monday morning I arrived at school, jaded but
determined. I had a meeting with my teacher
after class and he gave me a piece of paper
with some statements on it, told me to learn
them, and write them on a blank page before
I started doing anything with an exam.

"Before you answer the question read your
list. Ask yourself which statement relates to
the question? Then and only then begin to
answer the question."

Did I pass the next exam? Absolutely. We were
both pleased and I have used that technique
to help myself and other learners ever since.

It kept me focused. It enabled my mind to recognize something familiar in an unfamiliar (exam) situation, and a situation which is quite a tense one for me.

<u>What were the statements?</u>

What is the question asking you to do?

Who does the question relate to?

Where is the piece taking place?

How did this affect the person or effect the story/outcome/event/situation.

These statements can be used for any subject not just English, and for any situation not just exams.

I have used these questions when I am, preparing a tutoring session or presentation, writing a script or a book, attending a meeting.

The more focused you are the more pragmatic you become, and the better the communication of the information you need to share, or record is released.

My English teacher helped me to know success not just once, but over and over again. The result is I no longer fear exams or learning. I know I can be successful so I stretch myself further, and I am experiencing more success.

The way we feel about things

The fear of failure has been an uncomfortable companion of mine for way too long, now I no longer accommodate it. I have kicked it off the manifest, and travel more happily along without it. Am I successful with everything I do? No certainly not, not at first anyway, but I continue to do things anyway. I ask for help. I do research. I continue to try things to get to where I need to be. I need to be where I can help others, and I am loving doing that. Seeing people grow and succeed is the most rewarding thing for me, and although I am not helping as many people as I would like to yet, those I am helping already are helping me to realise my dream has already come true in this regard. I am very happy. The scale of that event is not up to me. I just need to be happy with what I am doing now, and keep turning up and doing it.

I have done this with my writing. My dream job has two parts. Writing and empowering people.

Recently I have tried to combine the two

together by writing self helps books.

When I am writing I am in my ideal state doing my ideal job and loving it so much it never feels like work. I use words to create pictures for people in the same way as Picasso used paint, texture, and light, to share his view of the world in his paintings, or Vivaldi used music to bring his view of the world to life.

Writing is me. Words are in me and they need to get out and live.

When we feel passionately about something we need to act. These feelings are coming from within us to help us grow as people, and to live well and happily.

This is also true for negative feelings. If I am feeling that a person is not acting in my best interests, then I need to heed that message and move away from, or stop being gulled by that person.

In families this is very hard to do. We love our family members to the point where we may let them get away with more than we would let other people get away with things, and for longer, but if your inner voice is telling you it is not okay then it is not okay.

Remove yourself from the situation if you can,

put distance between yourself and the person you feel uncomfortable with. If things have progressed even further to the point something has happened tell someone you trust. Do not hold onto this and say nothing. This will not only have happened to you. You will not be the only one who feels this way around that person, or people.

Only recently did a person I have known for years confide in me about a family member who had tried some unseemly behaviour with her in her younger years. Fifty years on and this lady still distances herself from this man, and so do many younger and older members of her family, so these things do happen. They can happen anywhere. In families. In the workplace. In schools. In hospitals and rest homes. At large gatherings. Among friends. With complete strangers. They can happen to anyone. Male and female. Young and old. Be on guard and keep yourself safe.

This covers a range of situations such as intimidation, bullying, sexual and financial harm to others to name a few.

If it doesn't feel right. It is NOT right.

A sprinkling of love goes a long way

Love is also a feeling. When we love
something, love doing something, or love
someone, we can't wait to be in that situation
or with that person. Our thoughts go back to
the person, or thing we love or love to do. It
could be a new car. Every time you see the
car, you love it. You may not own it yet, but
you still love it, and the more you love it the
more you will see it, and every time you will
feel love for this car. Love is a tangible thing,
as I mention in my book "Airbags and Starting
Over." It is real. You can see it as well as feel
it. When you go into a room full of love you
feel light. Love draws you in.

Falling in love is a feeling as well. When you
are falling in love you are feeling love, feeling
happy, and feeling good.

Being loved is a different thing altogether.
This comes to you and is received by you, and
there is a mutual connection involved. Being
loved is the best feeling in the world, and does
not rely on romantic or sexual attraction to be
in force.

One of my workplaces is a Marae.   A Marae is
a place where Maori people gather and
welcome all people to them.

When I first started working there I felt I was a

visitor. Over time a short time as it happens, I have come to love being there. I love going there. I love tutoring there. I love the people there. It is the highlight of my working week to be there, and fantastic things are happening there. Working with a group of committed and successful people is a joy and the place emanates joy. From a building with a few people in it every week to a vibrant meeting place with cars in the car park every day is a testament to the love of and for the people, working to grow in their families, jobs and community. With love working like this in practical ways, it brings more people in and more growth occurs.

Love with action turns the corner every time. If you love someone or something and take action you will be rewarded beyond your wildest dreams. Sometimes the action you need to take is to love someone unconditionally. This means keep loving them even if you are not around them. Love is a force and it is powerful. You can use love always, and love always results in good. You can even love people who have not served you well. Love the person not what they have done. Make sure in this scenario that you are not around them, if it is not in your best interest.

Many addicts who go through a rehabilitation

process will revisit those they have affected in their past. This is an acknowledgement for them that their behaviour was not all right, and affected others in a negative way.

Likewise some offenders acknowledge the error of their ways, choices or actions, and take steps to correct those behaviours.

Know that if you have had a bad experience at the hands of another person you, can walk away and stay away to keep yourself safe, and that is perfectly all right. You are not judging the other person, you are working with your inner voice, to keep yourself free from further harm.

Many people have lost vast amounts of money at the hands of seemingly reputable financial advisors or businessman. Does this mean you shouldn't invest money again in the future? No it means you may need to invest your money somewhere, or with someone else where the return is lower, but your money will still be there for you.

This is what you need to ask yourself. Can I afford to lose this money?

Remind yourself when you are getting the spin "This is my/our money."

Remember it is very easy to spend someone

else's money, and to the person who is handling your money, you are that someone else. What they want is to make money off your money, and for them, they, will always find the someone else, who will fall for the spin, so if it doesn't feel right? That's right. Don't do it. Be guided by your inner voice. I am listening to mine big time these days. Why? Because it has not been wrong yet. Ignore it to your peril.

Chapter 9. Frustrations

As I write this I am experiencing a very real frustration. Our internet connection is not allowing us to be connected. This is a frustration because on the weekends I like to research material for my writing, and without internet access this makes that task extremely difficult.

We pay for the service which of late has not been stable, and this is across all providers not just ours. We pay our bill on time. We have filters. We follow instructions by turning the modem off, waiting the recommended time. Shut down the computer, restart the computer, turn the modem on, but when this continually happens multiple times a day clearly there is an infrastructure or cabling problem. My issue here is that they (the provider) won't be honest and just say we are having issues with the cable in your area.

You phone for assistance, and you are the one treated as the problem while being charged for a service you are not receiving. Is this ok? No.

For me what makes this worse is not the lack of service that is provided. It is that staff are told to lie or are giving out misinformation to customers. The provider knows there is a problem across multiple households in the same area, are we all doing exactly the same thing wrong? No.

When I am confronted with a response that I know is crafted to stall or not address an issue up front, and that is the biggest frustration of all for me. I can do two things: I can take it out on the person on the end of the phone who is doing their job, or I can hang up and not inflame the situation.

Given that I knew there was an issue I hung up. Don't confuse this action with giving up. We will be receiving the monthly bill soon and I will be advising the company that we are not paying for service on the following dates, because we didn't receive the service billed for. I am quite sure we will get a response quite different to the spin we are getting over the phone.

I am bringing this up here because we seem to be living in a world where frustrations spill over to anger because we feel we are not being heard or listened to.

Then just as I sit down to start the next chapter the following day emblazoned across the television news "IP Provider hacked thousands of customers without service. This started earlier in the week in smaller areas and is now more widespread......."

So there it was, the truth out there finally.

I am in a line of work where I deal with people who experience real consequences in these situations.

They react inappropriately or as some would say over the top. Why? Because someone has either; not done what they were instructed to do, or have not done what they had told them they would do, or not listened to the person properly and chosen to do nothing. Fobbed them off in other words.

This may seem trivial on the surface, but I can assure you when you take someone at their word and their action or inaction doesn't result in the outcome you expected, that creates an issue for you, and generally speaking people do react to that.

A tragic outcome in a small community in our country was the result of a person being told a matter was being sorted and nothing seemed to be happening for that person.

Now it is not as easy as saying the staff weren't doing anything, or not doing their jobs properly. Obviously an investigation is taking place and it may well find that the staff did all they could.

We live in a place where streamlining services means a lot of money gets spent on Technology solutions (Computer Software Programmes) at the expense of people. Many people are being put out of work, and the public are being told they are being replaced by Technology. This may well be true, but it is only one part of the problem.

When you take staff away from a place, and then you increase the workload of those who remain, there is going to be real consequences.

People can only work within the system they have to operate in, and when that system is not properly resourced people are affected.

It is important to realise that if you are being

affected, you need to take action that protects you, and the person you are working or dealing with.

Ask the person if you can record the conversation. If that is not allowed, take notes and follow those up with an email or letter to the person to make sure that what you heard is what was said to you and that the person is acknowledging the action agreed to is taking place. This follow up can act as a reminder for the person.

What are you hearing these days?

We have looked at active listening briefly in an earlier chapter, but a real life situation highlighted this so I am adding it here.

A guest speaker was addressing a group on a topical issue. I was there with material on the topic as well. The discussion was progressing well until one of the people in the group brought up the role of parents into the equation. The whole tone of the discussion changed. People launched in saying you can't say that. The speaker said "If you let me finish I can explain what I mean."

The body language around the group told me that two of the six people would listen and I was right. The other three people switched off or couldn't get passed the 'Blame the parent' angle they perceived had been put forward. One person wasn't engaged at all and had to leave early anyway.

Things started to become heated I intervened and handed out the written material I had prepared earlier on the topic. The speaker who is knowledgeable on the topic was trying to share his knowledge, to explain away some common misconceptions.

After a break, with time for the people to read the material that I handed out, we got back to some very good discussion about misinformation that is in the public domain, and all parties were satisfied.

If you are not sure that what you have been saying has been heard, you can ask the person "Did you just say?" or "Have I heard this right?" Ask a question which clarifies what is being said.

This is useful for situations such as meeting with a teacher, a staff meeting, meeting with your supervisor, employer, human resource people, helping customers, when seeing the doctor or a lawyer, your teacher , tutor or lecturer, your minister, visiting the council with a request, dealing with, the police, funeral director, a welfare or any other agency.

We take baggage with us when we go to these

meetings or places, and we need to, dare I say it, de-clutter before we arrive. If we don't we can miss valuable information, or take the wrong meaning into what is actually being said, or impart the wrong information to the person in the first place.

I know I have mentioned something similar to this already but given that how we communicate is primarily through the auditory system speaking and listening we need to get both parts working properly. Be present. Don't go off into your own thoughts. Stay focused.

What are you saying and how are you saying it?

How we say something is not just about our tone or volume. Our whole body is speaking when we are communicating.

When someone you know well is lying to you how do you know they are lying?

The words are falling out of their mouth perfectly fine. Their diction is usually good. They know what they are saying, and make sure you get a clear message so how do you know they are lying to you?

Body language? Maybe they are not looking

directly at you? Maybe they are being to precise giving you too much information? Perhaps they are not as relaxed as they would normally be?

When you find yourself out of your depth and you try to fit in, or get something you really want, the way you communicate will be different than when you are comfortable.

We let off vibes. We can be seen as intense or aggressive. We may not be very relaxed in the situation. Why is this?

I think it is partly because we see ourselves as being vulnerable or exposed. I also think we spend way too much time thinking about what will happen if we are turned down or turned away.

I have grappled with this myself. These days I focus on the great time I had with xyz even though I may not know them all that well.

I see the positive outcomes to my requests. Even if the answer is no at that time, that does not mean the outcome is negative. The timing may not be right and a better result may come later.

I have an "I am thankful for the positive outcome" approach before the situation. Followed up with "I am happy with the outcome" philosophy with me as I go into the situation, and I continue with the, "I am thankful for the positive outcome" attitude at the conclusion of the meeting or event.

What I have found since I started doing this, is that I am more relaxed regardless. More relaxed, more open, more effective.

I know it seems too easy. Try it and see if it works for you.

I have to go to the Doctor's next week so I will be practicing what I preach here. Can't say I have had all good experiences with the Doctor in the past, however this time will be quite different to previous experiences. Why? "I am thankful for the positive outcome."

What we tell ourselves

I had a really great conversation with a lady I know who has battled to give up smoking for over eighteen months. This lady has tried lots of methods, one of which came with a book which she had read to no avail.

She had done most of the things in the book, but still the need to smoke overtook her.

Then recently she decided she had to get on top of her smoking and stop it. She read the book again and read a sentence which said "you just tell yourself you don't smoke anymore."

Up until this point she had been going for a walk if she felt like a cigarette, or had a coffee, or watched a movie. Exchanged the cigarette for something else, and for her this did not work.

When she felt like a cigarette she said to herself, "You don't smoke anymore.", then carried on with what she was doing. As amazing as this may sound it has worked for her. Why? Well as she said she had been telling herself she needed to smoke for years, and now she no longer smokes.

She has changed the message, and the new message is becoming the thing that is happening now.

Anyone who has seen my picture in this book, or who knows me will tell you I am not the smallest person. For some reason my body likes to hold onto weight. I am understanding this more now, and I too am changing the message on this issue. "I no longer need to hold onto the weight."

For me it is no longer about getting rid of the weight as if the weight is the issue. It has become about letting my body know, that I no longer need the weight to protect me.

How do you right a wrong?

Sometimes we get caught up in trying to put things right, or wait for something to be put right, and we end up with disappointment as a companion.

If you have done all you can to put the wrong you created right you need to accept that you have done your best and leave it behind you. It is done. You cannot undo it. That's a fact.

I do cover this subject in "Airbags and Starting Over" for those of you have read that book this is a reminder/refresher you choose.

If someone has done you a wrong and you are waiting for them to put that right stop waiting. Love the person anyway and move on. Don't give the disappointment any energy at all. Why?

Energy is powerful and grows if you give it life and the result is the disappointment grows. Your perceptions of the person and or situation becomes more negative, and you find yourself in a spiral going nowhere positive at all.

Did you do it?

Did you add to it?

If the answer is no you are off the hook.

Did you go blindly along with it?

Did you expect it of that person?

Did you see it coming?

If the answer is no go back and look for the signs that would have been there. You need to be honest for this to work. Things like "The same thing happened to.... or I never thought they would do that to me...." are both indicators that you should have been awake to the person's behaviour.

Where are you with all this now?

Are you angry?

Feeling used?

Feeling duped?

Feeling guilty that you didn't see it coming?

Replay what happened in your mind and give yourself a different ending.

You may need to do this a few times, but it will leave you with a calmer feeling about the person/event and as the outcome is different the heat will go out of the situation. No heat, no life. Move on cleanly without it.

Before you say easy for her to say, (I know you are thinking it.) I have done this to great effect, and am reaping the benefits. So try it and see.

Easy? No, but as with all new things it has become easier the more I do it.

Chapter 10. I Love Tulips

Yes. Tulips are my flowers of choice. They come into full bloom for my birthday every year. I love the vibrancy of them. They are one of the few flowers that keep growing when you put them into water.

Why am I bringing up Tulips here?

Tulips are my sign. The sign that my life is on track and progressing. I look for them and they find me in all sorts of situations.

When the house our son and grandchildren were living in was burned down, just prior to us staying with them, our older son and family accommodated us in a town a bit further away. This was a very sad time and came very soon after my mother in law had passed away right on our family Christmas celebrations. My Mum's furniture was in the house that had burned down. My mum had passed away two years before, so the fire took away precious memories that had been relocated for practical use, as well as having sentimental value. After weeks of boarding with friends a house became available for them to shift into on the 26th of December. Boxing Day a public holiday in this country. Everyone of course was pleased at this fortunate turn of events, because just a week prior there was still no suitable housing available in the town for our family members of the burned out house.

We were able to assist with the shift which went smoothly. Replacement items were delivered on the day. Beds assembled and made up. Takeaway food for dinner a real treat for the grandchildren who were very good when the shift was in progress.

My mum did tapestry and all the grandchildren had a framed tapestry done by her on their wall. Our son was no different. He worked with his insurance assessor, and the tapestry was sent away to see if it could be restored.

While we were staying with him he brought home a set of Tulip paintings over three canvasses and put them on his lounge wall. They immediately calmed my sense of reawakened loss and just before we left at the end of our time with family for our long drive back home to Invercargill, he gave me a set the same which hangs in my hall.

I just knew when he brought the Tulips into the house that things would work out well even though they had lost everything, and it did.

And yes the tapestry has been restored and hangs proudly on his wall once again.

Supporting the local church fair we walked around the hall and my husband found a small lantern with Tulips on it which now sits on my lounge cabinet. I look at it often and smile, that had not been a good week for me at work, but the following week went much more smoothly.

Coincidence? I don't believe so.

Find something that brings you joy. Whether it is in season or not. You may find it will appear just when you need it to, to brighten up your day, or confirm that what you are doing is the right thing to do, and will work out.

Being aware

Often when we occupy a space or place that is not happy we become aware of all the negative or bad things around us, and this tends to amplify the unhappiness we are experiencing.

When things are going well we tend to become complacent and forget to be aware of all the other good things that are around us. Why is this?

Well we are coasting and when we coast we drift, and tend to drift away from where we need to be.

Let's think about a journey, and on this journey we are in a vehicle. The weather is wet with the wind gusting at times. What is the driver doing?

The driver is being vigilante. The driver is using the windscreen wipers to clear the water from the windscreen to maximize the view of the road ahead.

The driver is alert to the feel of the car on the road with the wind gusting, and is holding the steering wheel to keep the car positioned correctly on the road, as well as driving at a speed that takes into account the driving conditions of the road.

Why is the driver doing all these things?

To keep the driver, passengers and other road users safe.

Now picture this. You are on a journey. It is a summers' day and you are going to a holiday destination. People have been looking forward to this journey. There is a real buzz in the vehicle. People are laughing and chatting, playing games even singing. The road is dry. The Air Conditioner is on and everyone is travelling in comfort. The driver is driving along and taking note of the other traffic, the scenery and.......

Is the driver driving safely? Yes

Is the driver aware of his surroundings? Yes

Is the driver on guard?

Now you may be saying to yourself or thinking, of course the driver is. But why would the driver be on guard? Where is the heightened risk?

Of course when you are on a journey there is always risk, but how much determines the actions and awareness of the driver, and everyone else in the vehicle.

Now pause, take a moment to think about the wet, windy journey. See yourself in that vehicle. Can you hear the wind? What does the road sound like? What is the view like out of your window with the rain coming towards your vehicle? What does the road look like? What do the passing houses or scenery look like? How does it feel? Do you feel cold? Scared? Apprehensive? Do you want to just get to your destination and get out of the vehicle? Do you want to pull over and stop until the weather improves?

Ask yourself how aware am I in this vehicle?

Now pause and take a moment and think about getting into a vehicle with all your holiday stuff loaded into the back of the vehicle ready for you to use when you get out at your destination. You have your favourite music playing quietly in the background, you are chatting with your friends or family about what you are looking forward to doing over the coming days. The sun is streaming in the windows. The day is clear. The traffic is moving along nicely there is an air of fun in the vehicle. You hear lots of chatter and laughter going on including the driver who is involved in the conversation. You are relaxed, and happy. The scenery is unfolding the further along the road you travel. What are you saying? What are you doing? How aware are you of the road ahead? How are you feeling? Relaxed? Excited? At ease? Not a care in the world?

Now ask yourself and be honest. How aware are you in this vehicle?

I don't know about you, but when I am a passenger in a vehicle going somewhere I want to get to on a sunny day, I tend to chill out completely. I am not at all aware of the road. In fact I have been known to wonder how we got to a town so quickly, because I have not been paying that much attention to the landscape sliding by my window at all. I often get lost in my own thoughts.

Why? I am not as aware. I am lulled into a false sense of security because all around me looks well, feels well so I think it is well.

This is exactly what drifting is. We lose awareness. We lose traction. We coast along and stop paying attention, or being grateful for all the good things we have in our lives.

I have my tulips around me so I know that I have plenty of things, people and love in my life to be grateful for and I am grateful every day.

The latest addition, a much needed new bed, and yes my husband saw a headboard with a stained glass tulip on it so that was purchased to go with the bed. Was the headboard the dearest one in the shop? No it was cheaper than the matching headboard for the bed and

I love it.

I have learned and am a firm believer in being aware when things, people, work, and love are good. The more aware you are of the good things, the more good things will arrive and show up, and that is a fantastic way to spend your day.

Even in the days of sadness or sorrow look for the good things or remember the good things in your life and be aware of them. I can tell you that by doing so it will help you through those sad, sorrowful times.

It doesn't stop them but it will soften their impact on you.

Stress

Recently the topic of stress came up in conversation. A lady I know had been on a seminar and had to fill in a worksheet on how she handled stress.

Now this lady doesn't buy into stress and was told that everyone has stress and she had to fill in the form. Quite perplexed she said "Actually having to fill this form in could nearly cause me stress." This caused a few giggles around the room because people in general have an aversion or dislike of filling out forms.

What transpired from this was the belief this lady had around stress. She firmly believes there is no place for stress in fact she quotes the Bible as saying "not to become a slave to our thoughts."

Situations occur. Losing your job, going through a divorce, being ill, supporting someone who is suffering. All these situations happen in life to us or those we love or care about, but it is how we see, think, or feel about these things that determine whether or not we are stressed.

We can choose to replay the thoughts, and/or feelings we have around these situations, or we can choose to see the situation and work out how we are going to deal with it. The less we think about it and get caught up in our feelings about it, the quicker the solution will appear, and the situation will be resolved and gone from our consciousness.

Yes this does work. Yes it takes practice. We can choose to give stress a long life, a short life or no life at all.

What choices have you made?

What is a better choice for you to make?

Be aware. Take a risk. Do something that is better for you. Work towards a stress free life.

The best antidote to stress is being grateful for everything.

The way I do that is to surround myself with yes, Tulips my sign that no matter how bad things may appear to be right at that moment, I have a visual reminder of all the good things I have, and am grateful for them.

I am blessed my Tulips keep me on track when I get up in the morning, go to sleep at night, in my environment at work and around my home to keep me aware of all the good things I have in my life.

I hope you can find something that keeps you aware of all the good things in your life past and present. Add gratitude and enjoy a win, win situation.

Chapter 11. Staying the course

Yes this is the point you have (hopefully) arrived at. The daily grind. Keep at it. Stand firm. Be focused daily no matter what part of the process you are currently in.

Why?

Simply put, because it is the commitment, dedication and unwavering belief that will sustain you, move you to your goal and bring it home.

Faith

Yes the one thing we can state truly to ourselves, friends, family, and the world that no one actually sees. Just like a few other things that make the world tick and improve our lot and the lot of others. Gravity. No one can see gravity. Electricity. No one can see electricity. Air. No one can see air. Dreams. Only you can see your dreams no one else.

I bring this up here because we have dream or goal stompers amongst us and they love nothing better than to show up and undermine what you are doing. The only weapon they need to derail you is words. All you gave to do is listen, and yes the seeds of doubt are sown. Be firm in your resolve.

You are in the process of amazing change for you. To better you. Your faith in you needs to be absolute. Only you can bring the change home. No one else.

That's right it is completely up to you so stay focused on the good. The good you want. The good you deserve. The good things you can do, with the good you receive, and expect the good to arrive no matter what.

That's right no matter what.

This is where daily faith is paramount. Things break. Negative things happen to or around you every day. People say negative things. You may have done something great, and a colleague, group or family member can only find a flaw, or make a comment that is disparaging, and if you focus on that you have derailed yourself.

Yes that's right. You have derailed yourself.

Now you may be reading this thinking how can that be? The other person said those things not me.

You would be right. They said those things. Think about this. Did you hear them or did you listen?

You see if you listened to those negative things you gave them a breath of air and they began breathing. Living. You then think on them.

How to turn this around then? Quite simply just say this.

"I hear you, but in spite of that small thing you found, I've done an amazing job of it."

Then smile and get on with your day. Keep looking for the good. Acknowledging the good. Enjoying the good and yes the good will continue to show up.

I don't know about you but I would much rather have the good turning up.

Mixing things up

Just like a family favourite recipe sometimes you need to either add something to it, or have something exciting alongside it, to keep the diners interested in the meal you are serving up over and over again.

The family roast is one of those dishes. The meat may always be the same, but the vegetables change with the seasons, so too can the gravy or the pudding/dessert.

We also need to be mindful of what we are doing. We can have a good routine which gets us through the days and or nights, but every now and then, it is good to mix things up. Why? Well opportunity has a way of turning up when you least expect it, and that is often when we do something a little different, at a different place, or in a different situation.

So be open to adding things to your life and mixing them in. You may be pleasantly surprised at the outcome.

Conversely if you struggle with someone or something at a particular time, see if you can change the time so you don't have to deal with them, or a for a time that is better for you, earlier or later in the day. You may find it is not the other person who is the issue, you may be simply too tired or anxious at that time of the day/night to deal with them.

If the base recipe is good why change it? You don't have to, is the short answer, but if the accompaniments are tired you can certainly do something about them.

Take a bedroom. If you change the furniture around you can change the whole look and feel of the room. You can take pieces out. Add pieces. Change the colour scheme. The room is still there and working isn't it?

Don't be afraid to mix things up from time to time. This will stretch you, and you can always change things back if you don't like the result or try something else.

I found starting with small things made it easier. I am quite a bit bolder now, and I am finding that the more I stretch myself, the more I grow, the better, things are for me.

Torchlight

Yes even I am in need of a torch from time to time to light my way. When my husband is asleep in our room, and I need to find something in the dark. When the power goes out. There is nothing wrong with having a torch to hand. What is essential though is to have the batteries in good working order. Having flat batteries in a torch is going to at best, light the way dimly or not at all.

We can find ourselves at times unexpectedly in need of guidance or direction with no torch, or seemingly no one on hand to help us through. What to do?

I have found and please do not laugh at this.
I have found that by pretending I am the other
person I can look more objectively at the
situation and then find a solution to my issue.

Under no circumstances begin to panic.
There is a saying and it goes like this "What
would Jesus do?"

The saying is there so you never feel alone or
overwhelmed by events large or small,
changing or unknown, and you act in an
honourable way.

Putting your mind onto what another may do
also gives you breathing space. It stops you
reacting without thought attached to your
action.

There are many practices out there that also
can help in situations that you find yourself in
or around that will keep you calm and enable
a better result for you. Tapping.
Ho'oponopono. Prayer. Meditation.

I encourage you to do some research and find
a torch that works for you.

Remember that God has created us. He has
provided tools for us to be the best we can be
in all situations.

Chugging along

Once we have learned to stay the course which is simply turning up and doing right by ourselves and others, all we need to do then is keep chugging along.

Sir Edmund Hilary was asked in a radio interview many years ago soon after he had climbed Mount Everest, how he had kept going to the top of Mount Everest when so many others had failed. The tone of his voice softened, and there was a hint of humor in it when he said "the same way I got to the first station, one foot in front of the other, and then we were there. Tenzing and I."

Chugging along is what gets you lined up for the end, for the goal which is in reach, you've done everything you need to do, and there it is in plain sight.

Quite often it is at this point one of two things may occur. A major upset, or complacency shows up, and the result may well be that you can see the goal, but even though you are chugging you don't seem to be getting any closer to it.

In these situations I really push myself through this phase, because this is the point, the final point on the journey that allows me to arrive at the destination I set out to get to.

99

The extra effort confirms I am totally committed to the goal I have set, and once I have got there I may need to learn a few more things, but I know having achieved the goal, I can be successful in whatever comes in relation to it after that.

Gobbledegook?

Let's look at a job. I want to get a more challenging job in the company I work for. I see a position advertised that I want to do. It is different to what I am doing now. The role I am in is going well and it is good for the company to keep me in that role. How do I give myself the best possible shot at the new position I want.

Research. I find out what that job is really about. I talk to people who have done it in the past. I break down the advertisement for it. I ask for the job description. I make a checklist of what I expect the job to be and my role in it.

I line up my current skills, in my current job alongside the job description. I look to other skills I have, and see how they fit. I put all this information in the job application.

Then I start working on the interview and what I am going to say. I make sure I have questions to ask at the interview. I make sure I have facts about the company in relation to that role, and how I can be of benefit to that company in that role. I am willing to do training to enhance my effectiveness for the company in that role.

The day arrives when I am offered the job. It is at this point that some people have a rethink and decide not to do the job. There may have been something said in the interview stage that has put them off.

If you find yourself in that situation go over your checklist and be sure. Once you are sure you no longer want the position or you realise the position is not actually what you thought it was, remove yourself from contention before they offer the position to you.

When you are offered the position go back to your checklist and accept the job knowing you have the skills, you have learned skills to get to where you are now. Know that you can learn more skills for the position you now have. You have met your goal and you now get on with the new position. Be firm in your resolve. Enjoy your success.

Chapter 12. Acceptance

We usually hear about acceptance when something of a negative or unforeseen event has occurred. We are almost primed from an early age that we must just accept whatever has happened and get on with things.

Recently a colleague went through a very traumatic marriage break up. It was traumatic because it broke down so quickly, there weren't many warning signs, and the partner moved onto another swiftly.

There has been a lot of talk around how long is it going to take for this person to accept it and get on.

Well where loss involving someone you love and trusted is involved, it is not like a television episode where in a few weeks everything is resolved and you just get on. For some people it can take a significant amount of time to work through all the stages of grief before they can be in a place where they just get on.

We need to be mindful of this when something negative happens.

We need to be mindful too when something positive happens for, or to people. Not everyone reacts to a positive situation in the way they or we may expect.

Take Lottery winners. Statistics tell us that many people who win the Lottery are no better off two years after they were, when they won the Lottery.

People who get promotions often are not satisfied, and start applying for other positions when they have barely got their feet settled in the job they just took over.

What does this have to do with acceptance?

It is all part of a process.

To get to acceptance you have to understand that once you have reached the point of acceptance, you need to add gratitude and continue on your journey.

Arriving at the point of acceptance doesn't mean you stop.

Some people who are given much, keep, expecting more, and they get it time and time again. Why?

They are grateful for what they receive. They accept it. They feel good about what they receive, and they continue accepting it.

Now you may be sitting there reading this thinking, well why wouldn't they? If they are getting what they want of course they are going to keep accepting it. Who wouldn't?

Well it is not that long ago that I was tied up in litigation, and I was not getting what I wanted out of the experience at all. I felt I was hitting my head against a brick wall even though the facts were there, and I had done nothing wrong. I was extremely stressed and more so when I lost and had to face the fact that money was going out rather than coming to me. The feelings that started swirling were so intense I took a deep breath and decided to accept it all. I had done my best. I had been honest throughout, and for whatever reason I had lost. I forgave those involved, and began a life without the litigation in it.

I could have sat down defeated and feeling sorry for myself kept living in the injustice and disappointment of it all, but that would not have changed the result. I accepted it was over, and even though others wanted to have another round it was over for me. I accepted that and moved on.

The odd thing about life is that sometimes we get the justice for something in unexpected ways, and this has happened for me recently.

I lost in litigation, but the truth has finally come out, and I am no longer seen as the perpetrator but as the victim.

Now you may be asking yourself what has all this got to do with acceptance?

I believe that by accepting the loss and forgiving all those involved, I stepped out of the way, which took the life out of my negative thoughts and feelings, which then enabled others to get the true picture.

What I have found is once we accept things, other things around us settle or change. We see things differently. We feel different. We are in a better place.

When I am given praise for something I accept it, and I am grateful for it.

I used to feel embarrassed or not worthy of praise. To be honest I never received a lot of praise. Other people would often take my ideas and be rewarded or praised for them and

I suffered in silence. No more.

Many people find themselves in negative situation time and again and they accept that as their normal. Many people will say #### happens.

When they do this they are accepting there is not an alternative.

Being in a negative situation is NOT the same as accepting it. There is a very big difference.

If you are in a negative situation make a plan to get out of it. Accept you have the means and support to get out of it, and work towards that goal.

I was in a negative situation. I lost. I got out. I am free of it. The truth is now seen by those who needed to know it.

I am not defined by what occurred. I am continuing on with what I was doing prior and people are benefitting from what I am doing. I am helping people and meeting my original goal in spite of the negative situation that occurred.

I now know that I appreciate much more the work I am doing.

Do we have to rollover to get to acceptance

NO. This idea that people accept things because they are weak is a fallacy.

It takes strength of mind and character to reach the point of acceptance. Whether the situation is positive, or negative.

Why?

You are making a conscious decision. You know when you make the decision you need to live with the consequences of it.

For me it was walking away from round ....I had been in the ring fighting to clear my name for a long time. Walking away from the last round wasn't easy, but then the facts of a loss were sobering, and I knew I had been honest, and that the result did not reflect what had occurred.

Once I accepted it was over I left it completely. Even when it reared up again, I left it alone.

Often when we do reach acceptance there will be something that comes out of the blue, when you least expect it to do with situation.

What do we do then?

Well I have accepted the situation in its

entirety, and if there is another bit tagged on I accept that too, but I do not pick up the sword and fight another round.

When we accept good things into our lives the same thing happens. We can have received something really good, and we are feeling very blessed, and then out of the blue we receive something that we weren't expecting and it can be overwhelming.

Why should it feel overwhelming?

Well we seem to take longer learning how to receive good things that just come to us.

I was taught we have to earn everything good. The mantra we had growing up was "Good things come to those who wait."

Well I realised a few years ago that I was done waiting. Waiting for what? Good?

Good is only useful when it has arrived.

You see I was so busy waiting for it I found myself running out of time to receive it.

I was receiving the waiting not the good.

I decided I was going to receive the good. I didn't know how, but if the waiting kept showing up because I focused on the wait, logic told me the good would start turning up if I focused on that.

Well was I surprised when the good started showing up yes. I was shocked when it continued to arrive, and I felt unworthy of it to begin with because I was not used to it.

That's right I have had to get used to it, and that is getting easier every time I receive something good.

You see I don't have a problem doing good things. I never think twice about that, but receiving good things somewhere that was for 'other people'.

Now I am 'other people' to anyone who is not me, and so are you. So if you are doing good things for other people, and you want to receive good things, people, situations in your life, they will come, so long as you do not keep waiting for them.

You need to desire and expect good things to arrive, then get on with your life as if they are here already, they will show up, and when they do accept them. Be grateful for them. Be pleasantly surprised.

The Bob Proctor book "You were Born Rich" covers this very well.

Chapter 13. Worksheets and summing it all up

Worksheets for resolving issues

Focus on the Solution

Always have your solution box the biggest one. That is to be your focus. The Solution **NOT** the Issue. The issue has already happened or is in play and cannot be changed.

If there is an issue recurring you need to look at how it has occurred, then find a way to break the cycle. See where you could have altered something, or look at the situations from the solution you want, and track back the steps you will need to take to get it.

Ask yourself can you solve the issue in 3 steps?

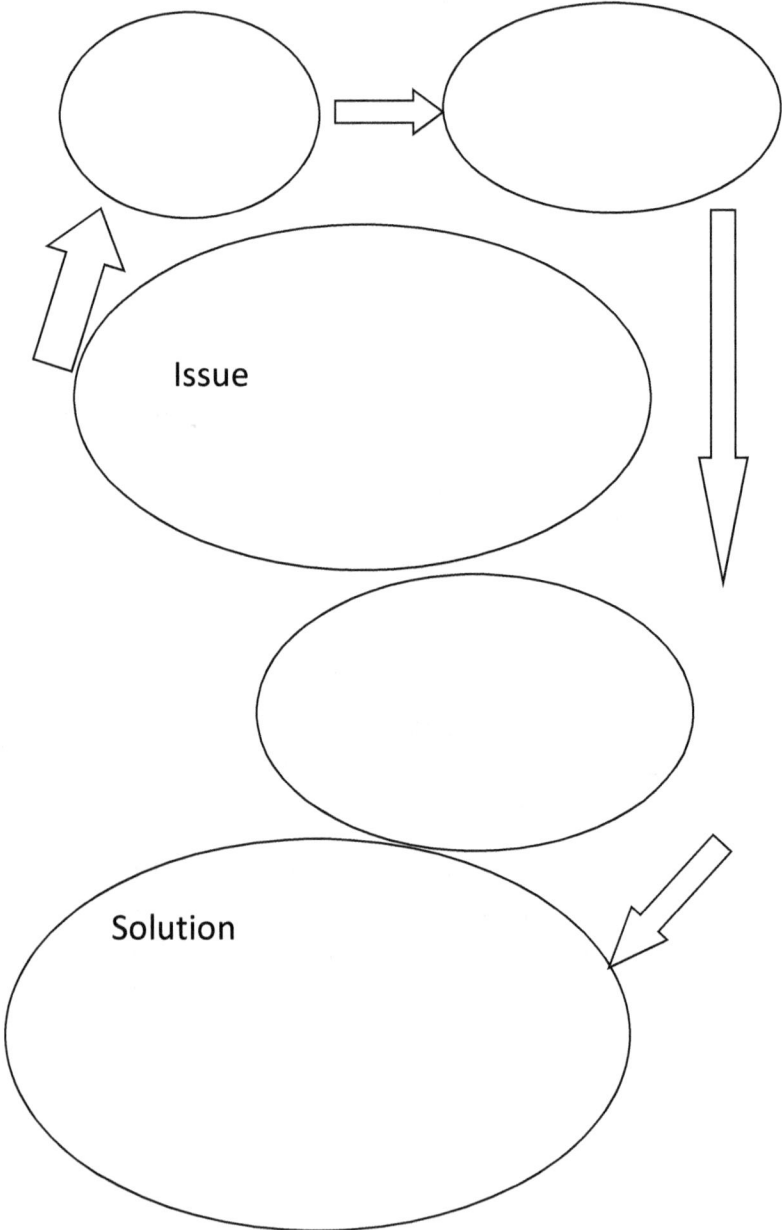

Issue

Solution

Empowerment

List three things you have set a goal for/or wanted to do and have done:

I have achieved	
I have achieved	
I have achieved	

List three things you have set a goal for/ or have wanted do and are doing now:

I can	
I can	
I can	

List three things you still want to do: Leave Blank

Fill in section one and two.

Fold your paper into three, with section one on the top, then fold in half covering over the writing. Give your paper to someone to hold for a day or put it in a safe place.

Get on with your day and do not think about it.

Go back to it the next day and open it up. Read the first section only.

How do you feel? Congratulate yourself. Be proud or yourself. Smile. A very big smile.

Now fold the paper down to reveal the next section. How likely are you to do these things now?

Fill in goals for the third section.

Fold your paper up with section two on the top. Fold the paper in half covering the writing and put aside.

Revisit each week.

Be honest with yourself. Challenge yourself by asking yourself.

How on track am I? Do I need to make changes?

If you get the wobbles, or self- doubt that may

derail you. Read section one again.

You are an achiever already, and remind
yourself you can do it.

How do you know you can?

You have already, and are quite capable of
achieving this as well.

Relax the solution will come to you.

Repeat the process until you have achieved all
your goals, and keep adding new ones.

Keep your goal sheets in a box, folder or
envelope and on the days when you think you
are not making progress, go to the sheets you
have filled in and have a look. You will see
your achievements. You will see your new
pattern of doing things. You are going to feel
much better.   You will feel successful,
because you are succeeding. You will be more
focused and driven and more will be achieved
by YOU.

Goals don't have to be difficult. Goals do need
to be realistic. The more you achieve your
goals, the more adventurous, competent and
confident you will become.

Trust me this works.

Three goals at a time is achievable don't

swamp yourself.

Stick with three and success is a guarantee.

Summing it all up

I have learned that I have control over my life. I have experienced growth, achievement, success and satisfaction in my personal and professional life. I have set and met goals along the way, and I am not finished yet. I have also experienced losses in my personal and professional life. Through it all I have emerged a stronger, richer and more fulfilled person than I was prior to the gains I have made and the losses I have sustained.

I have learned it is not only okay to expect good things, people, and situations in my life. They start showing up.

I have learned that when I set goals which are good for me, but also help other people they are achieved. I get a nudge here and there that keeps me on track. I get ideas that pop into my head.

I have learned to expect to meet the right people at the right time, every time.

I have learned to be very clear about what I want in my life, and I keep adding and deleting to that list until I have it about right.

I am taking great delight in walking through

life being proactive as I go.

I want to be a successful writer. The first stage of that journey is to write.

I have been given a second chance to know writing and other successes in my life, and I am accepting it all with gratitude and love.

I hope my personal journey inspires you to see you in a new way.

To work on you for a better result.

To love you.

To love others.

To accept love in your life.

To set goals.

To achieve them.

To be brave and dream.

To live in the world of make believe from time to time.

To accept the negative and positives in your life.

To desire, expect, then accept all the good things that will arrive.

To be courageous. It takes courage to change.

You can do it.

That is where my journey has brought me now
that I am back on the road again.

The road has changed for me. It is a smoother
one now, with very clear signposts. There is
the odd curve and hill, but I see them
differently now. I accept they are part of the
journey. Now they don't hinder me from
reaching my destination.

Be empowered.......

I wish you all the very best on your journey
and remember:

**"To Empower Others Is To Enrich Your
Life, and Allow Others to Know a Better
Life For Themselves and Others."**

ABOUT THE AUTHOR

KAREN PIVOTT is the author of *Self Help Books, Adult Fiction and Children's Fiction, is a published radio scriptwriter with HCJB Beyond the Call with Ron Cline series 2001. Radio Southland 2004 and 2005.* Published play write "Gavin's 21st." 2000 Nelson fringe art festival and literacy specialist. Karen lives in Invercargill New Zealand with her husband. Karen loves educating and inspiring people to improve their lives and the lives of all the people they connect with.

www.ingramcontent.com/pod-product-compliance
Lightning Source LLC
Chambersburg PA
CBHW061741020426
42331CB00006B/1315